This was my favorite book! —Amber (age 11)

The Diary of a Young Resister *is great reading for all ages. The surprise ending really touched my heart.* —Donna, pastor's wife

I felt like I was seeing life through Salina's eyes. I really enjoyed the story.
—Andrea (teenager)

Acclaim for *Quest for the Other Kingdom: The First Book of Journeys:*

"New and progressive ideas never have an easy start. This is the story of a kingdom that widely uses slavery, and the culture shock of a free woman who visits it. She tries to spread her message of a morally better way, but does not receive a warm reception. Meanwhile, a runaway slave wants to escape his bonds by reaching the shores of the nation that would not treat him as property—but the journey he attempts is one that is often fatal. A intriguing tale for young adult fantasy fans, *The First Book of Journeys* is highly recommended for community library young adult fiction collections." —*The Midwest Book Review*

"*The First Book of Journeys* is filled with spiritual and psychological insights derived from Linda Settles' personal journey on the Sea of Life. Her training as a counselor and her involvement with others who have also taken this journey is evident on the pages of every book she has written.

In this book, she writes of a young man who grows up in the City of Bondage. Perhaps you have been there. It is a place that presses you to contradict the values of your own heart. This city is filled with risk, and getting out of it requires much courage. There is no guarantee that the traveler will reach his desired destination even if he takes that risk and sails away on the good ship *Seeking*.

Recovery principles abound in *The Quest for the Other Kingdom*, as do spiritual concepts such as Truth and Grace, Mercy, and Good Works. Regret shows up as well, along with his companion, Suffering. The characters may seem so very familiar to you because you know them, you've experienced them… we all do. Follow Brae and the Messenger—your own journey will be enriched as you get to know your fellow travelers on the Sea of Life."

—Pastor Dale Hollin, Columbiaville, Michigan, Assembly of God

QUEST FOR THE OTHER KINGDOM

Diary of a Young Resister

Linda Settles

Edict House Publishing Group, LLC
Rustburg, Virginia

Diary of a Young Resister
(Quest for the Other Kingdom)
© 2008 by Linda Settles

All rights reserved. No portion of this book may be reproduced in whole or in part, by any means whatever, except for passages excerpted for purposes of review, without the prior written permission of the publisher. For information, or to order additional copies, please contact:

Edict House Publishing Group, LLC
Post Office Box 1304
Rustburg, VA 24588
Phone: 434-821-4005
www.EdictHouse.com
Email: edicthouse@hotmail.com

Edict House books are available for special promotions, premiums and bulk discounts.

Cover and book design by Elizabeth Petersen, Mendocino Graphics
Book production by Cypress House
Cover illustration by Steve Ferchaud © Linda Settles
Interior illustrations by Steve Ferchaud © Linda Settles
Leather image on cover © iStockphoto.com/Bill Noll

Publisher's Cataloging-in-Publication Data

Settles, Linda.
   Diary of a young resister / Linda Settles. — 1st ed. — Lynchburg, VA : Edict House, 2008.
     p. ; cm.
   (Quest for the other kingdom ; 2)
   ISBN: 978-0-9790238-2-8

Summary: Salina was 9 when the Messenger came to the Land of Lasciviousness. After he left the persecution began; but although she longs for peace, she would rather die than go back to the old ways. Coming of age in a restricted country will be a test of Salina's courage and her faith.

1. Fantasy fiction, American—Juvenile literature. 2. [Fantasy.]
I. Title. II. Series.
   PZ7.S5123 D53 2008   2008931253
   [E]—dc22   0809

First edition

2 4 6 8 9 7 5 3 1   Printed in the United States of America

*I dedicate this diary
to my beloved Miarrow,
who will always be a hero to me,*

*and to Miammi,
a wise and wondrous woman.*

My name is Salina. I was born in the Land of Lasciviousness nine years before the persecution began. My memories of those early days are happy because Miarrow, my beloved father, and Miammi, my mother, worked in the city, and we had friends who came often to sit beside our fire at the end of the day.

We did not know of the Messenger and the truths that he taught us. We had not heard of the Emperor Addar, supreme ruler over all kingdoms, and his son the Great King Immon. We knew very little, I suppose, but we loved much, and that seemed to make up for it.

I remember sitting beside the fire, leaning on Miarrow's broad chest, Miammi stroking my hair. I listened to the words of the Messenger, and even then I knew that life would never be the same, for always, in my early memories, it was as if a great and terrible shadow hovered over us, like a beast about to devour us while we slept.

The Messenger was taller than Miarrow, and stronger too, I believe. He spoke quietly, but his words carried deep into the secret places of our hearts. He touched our eyes with amber oil from his crystal vial, and even I, a child of nine summers, could see the chains that had wrapped themselves around us, all of us.

I hated the chains. It was not too burdensome for us to exchange our life of ease for one of service to Immon, for he was the only one powerful enough to free us from our chains.

Miarrow made this journal for me, and Miammi sewed it together with her own precious hands. The blood that stains the binding is Miammi's blood, shed when the sharp needle pierced her hand—not once but many times—as she sewed the pages into the journal that I hold in my hands.

"Write, little Salina," Miarrow said to me when he handed me this book on my tenth birthday. "Write daily as your life is lived, so that you will not forget the victories won and remember only the suffering."

And so I have done. This is my account of the suffering endured and the victories won during the days of Chief Sodomon, in the Land of Lasciviousness.

Diary of a Young Resister

 Machato

CHAPTER 1: AGE TEN

Dear Lenore,

It is hot today. Though it is early, the sunshine is warm on my face. The fingers of Machato reach through the treetops to bathe my favorite stone, which I call Helgotha, in its white-hot light.

Helgotha is almost as big as I am, and, unlike me, well rounded. Though Helgotha is hard on my bottom when I sit too long, I come here often to visit with Machato and Helgotha and to write in my journal, which I have named Lenore.

Lenore is a lovely name, don't you think? It makes me think of the whine of the wind through the trees, and the sound of wolves howling at Machita, the night twin of Machato.

I hope you are well today, Lenore, as am I, except for a faint rumble in my stomach. I don't know if it is hunger that complains inside me. Sometimes I think something else gnaws at my insides, especially when Miarrow seems sad, as he does tonight. He and Miammi whisper behind their curtain. They think I do not know, but I know. I always know.

Dear Lenore,

The grass is very green today. So much greener than yesterday. And the sky is blue, like the feathers of the malachite that fish in the streams where the river runs into the sea. Dazzling—that is the word Miarrow uses for such happy colors. They are dazzling.

The rains came last light and washed the jungle. Even as I slept, I could hear it beating down on the yellow straw that covers our shelter. I am glad Miarrow pitched it last week. I don't like the feel of water dripping down on me while I sleep—drip, drip, like the blood of a pig that has been slaughtered and slung upon the posts to drain. Miarrow knows this. He is a good father.

Dear Lenore,

I am sorry I could not come earlier. There was much work to do this morning, and Miammi needed my help. I suppose there will be guests at our fire tonight. Bolati whispered of such news to Demensi when we broke the fast in the morning. He always knows such things because he is old enough to sit with Miarrow at the council fire. Demensi never tells me anything, but I have good ears, and I listen while I sing. Demensi struts because he thinks he knows everything. He knows less than I do, but talks more.

Miarrow is quiet today. He wears a little frown on his forehead, though his eyes smile at me. He doesn't want me to worry. He pats me on the head as if I am still small. Perhaps I am rather small for my age, but in many ways I am older than my ten summers. Everyone says so. But I just smile at him and let him think that I do not know.

Miammi calls. I must go now.

Dear Lenore,

This morning there is a child in Surice's house who was not there yesterday. I saw him at dawn, standing tall against the morning light, his hair windblown as always. He held the child in his fragile arms and she clung to him as to a father. I am dying to know how she came to be there. Why does Miarrow always send me to bed before the guests arrive? Well, not always, only when the mysterious guests come, those who have no names.

Machato hides his face today. Perhaps he is gloomy like the elders and Miarrow. Miammi sings in a sad voice. She carried food to Surice's house just after daybreak. I heard her moving quietly about the house, her footsteps light. Miammi did not sing then. When she returned she tried to hide her tears. But I saw them.

Ode to Machato

If the earth is the footstool
Of the Emperor Addar
Then what are you? Perhaps you are
His plaything, His flaming orange ball
That he tosses high and lets fall
Into the morning sky. Perhaps he cools
With breezes of the night
Your fiery head, and bids you stay
At ease, while Machita takes a turn.

He reaches down from the lofty height
You've spurned, with long, dark fingers
Of the night, then he tosses you as a child might
Toss a toy into the sky, once more,
Where you grow bright. Caught on fire
By the friction of your skin
Breaking through space and time.
Perhaps you are the plaything of Addar
As he sits upon His throne and starts
A new day in the Kingdom of Adawm.

Dear Lenore,

Miammi and I just finished my lessons for today. She has been teaching me the skills of reading and writing since I was four. She said I must write a poem today and so I did. I hope you like it, though it is really Machato's poem.

Miammi says I am precocious. I would think that is something terrible—the word does not sound nice—but Miammi says it with such pride that I think it must be a good thing.

I met the child today. Her name is Sashay. Such a pretty name. Miammi brought her to our house this morning, just after Machato decided to get out of bed.

You must enjoy sleeping on such soft, fluffy clouds, Machato. I wish I could see everything as you do. From where you sit, we must look so very small. I wonder sometimes if you can even see us at all.

But you must, because sometimes you smile at me and I get all warm and happy. Especially when the rains have come and it is gray and gloomy, and then you come, creeping through the long limbs of the mamboni trees, and I want to stand up on top of Helgotha and sing!

Sashay is wandering, so I must go and fetch her. It is easy to get lost in the jungle, and there are many dangers there. Most who stray into the shadows between the great trees do not return. Demensi says that an evil monster lurks beyond our village, just waiting for dogs and foolish children to stumble into his lair. I believe Demensi likes to frighten small children. Still, I do not think I want to go there.

Dear Lenore,

It is an awful day. Someone came in the night and carried poor little Sashay away. Demensi says it was the monster in the shadows, but I don't believe him. I have never seen a monster, only lions and crocodiles and wolves.

I will miss Sashay, but I didn't let myself get too attached. I knew she wouldn't stay long—just like the others.

CHAPTER 2: AGE ELEVEN

Dear Lenore,

It is my birthday today. I am having a party. Machato must be happy, as I am, for he has smiled his brightest since early this morning. Even the shadows between the great trees seem less somber today, their sternness dispelled by the light of Machato's smile.

Helgotha hardly seems to change at all. She is warm, but just as hard today as always. Does my birthday make no difference to you, Helgotha?

My bottom was sore from sitting here so long yesterday. I wrote until my fingers ached, and then ripped out the pages and burned them in the fire. I am ashamed of my angry thoughts. Miarrow would have scolded me, and Miammi would have cried to think of her sweet child writing such words. But they don't know me as you do, Lenore. They don't see my face when anger claims it, and shadows, like the monsters of the jungle, twist my cheeks and pinch my lips together so that I do not shout the words that are in my head.

It is better that I write such words secretly and feed them to the fire as I did yesterday. Then they will rise on the wind—ashes, light as the down of a newborn dove. I watched them swirl upward. Did the ashes tickle your face, Machato, as they flew past? They will not stop, you know, until they reach the throne of the Great King Immon. He alone can read the words written on ashes.

Will you be angry with me, Immon, when you read my words? I think not. I think you would say the same words if you were a girl, like me. I am only eleven, but I have lived a long time.

Dear Lenore,

Miarrow and Miammi argued behind their curtain last night. I awoke late in the night to the sound of their voices. Machita peeked from behind her nest of clouds and winked at me when I stared at her. I tried not to hear my parents' heated words, but I could not resist listening. I hope Immon forgives those who trespass in this way.

Miarrow said that he must join his brothers. I did not know that he had any brothers. I have never seen them, and Miammi said that she feared he would die if he went with them. Why would Miarrow do something so dangerous and so mysterious? Miarrow is supposed to thatch roofs and build fires and make leather products as he always has. He is no warrior.

Miarrow was gone at first light this morning. Miammi does not sing as she bakes our bread in the stone oven.

O Great King Immon, if you do not like my words written on ashes, please forget that I wrote them and do not take Miarrow away in the jungle.

Perhaps a monster prowls in the shadows of the great trees after all. I miss you Miarrow. I miss Sashay. I don't like being eleven.

Dear Lenore,

Machato rose early this morning. Helgotha was warm long before I climbed on her back. Perhaps you were awakened on Machita's watch, as I was, by the sound of small voices crying in the jungle. I went to Miammi's bed and found her lying awake, eyes wide open, staring at the moldering straw above her head. I am sure her cheeks were wet, but she smiled at me and moved over so that I could lie beside her. I am sure she was missing Miarrow, as I was.

"Why are there children in the jungle, Miammi?" I asked her. She shook her head at me and said sternly, "You imagine too much, Salina. You know the cry of the wildcats when you hear them. Now go back to bed and go to sleep." But I do not believe her. I do know the sound of wildcats—and this was not their sound.

Miarrow did not return this morning. I am worried that the shadow monster got him.

Machato, if you see Immon, will you tell him for me that I did not mean the words I wrote on the ashes. Tell him that I will write him a new letter, a lovely one with pleasant thoughts. Maybe he will like that better.

Lenore,

Last night my dreams were better. I have seen no unfamiliar children, so I must have dreamed their cries in the jungle the night before. It is strange that dreams can seem so real.

Machato, you seem happy today. The light of your smile touched my face and woke me early, even before Miammi was up. You laid out sunbeams on my path all the way to Helgotha. Those streams of laughter that I can see but not hear have lifted my sadness. I will laugh with you today.

Miarrow came home sometime in the night. Be certain that you tell Machita that I said thank you for lighting the paths through the jungle so Miarrow could find his way home.

I stepped over the dirty clothing that Miarrow discarded on the floor last night. He must have been very tired because he is not usually so careless. In the early morning light I saw dark stains on Miarrow's pants. I will not say what I thought they were, but I will look again when Machato is fully awake and see if I was mistaken.

Helgotha, you seem especially unkind today. Perhaps it is not your fault. I have eaten little in the last two days, since Miarrow left with his brothers. I am bonier than before. I will bring my blanket tomorrow and spread it between us. I hope that you do not mind, but it is difficult to write properly when my skin is pinched between my sharp bones and your hard back.

Miarrow told Miammi that he is a soldier in the army of the Great King. I do not see any uniforms, but sometimes I hear distant drums, and wonder if there is going to be a war.

Great King Immon, I have written my letter, and Bolati promises to cast it into the fire tonight. I hope you are no longer offended with me.

Lenore,

I know it is early, for I am the only one stirring in our small village this morning. I can barely see the sky between the black branches cast against the rumbling clouds. Machato is still sleeping in his dark nest, and Machita has diminished to a small sliver of golden light. The smell of last night's fire hangs upon the warm, wet air.

Helgotha shines like a beacon in her whiteness against the gloom. She is cool this morning, but just as hard as yesterday.

I am disappointed that I did not get a second look at Miarrow's stained pants. They were no longer on the floor when I returned to our house. Miammi took a basket of clothing to the river, and I am sure the pants were among them. It was not Miammi's laundry day, so I am very curious about those dark stains.

Miarrow limps like a hobbled horse this morning. I asked him about it, and he said that he stumbled over something in the shadows of the jungle. I asked if I could see his injury, and he became quite gruff. I wanted to persist, but his unusually stern face warned me that I should not.

There are two unfamiliar children at Surice's house today. I heard one, a little girl, crying in the night. Miammi prepared extra food last night that she will take to Surice's house for them today. She did not tell me this, but I know these things. Bolati made good on his promise to cast my letter into the fire. He said the ashes flew upward with a shower of sparks that was spectacular. Actually, Bolati did not use that last word because he has a limited vocabulary.

Miammi continues to provide books for me and give me hours every day to use them because she is convinced I will be a person of great influence someday. She says I am brighter than most. I do not see myself that way. Machato is bright, and even Machita is somewhat bright. I am dull. Eleven is the most boring of all my years. Not that I have had so many of them.

Lenore,

I met the children at Surice's house today. Yes, I am writing twice in one day—because I am so excited I cannot hold it all in. The boy is older than I. You would not know it, for he is even smaller than I am right now; he has had little to eat for months. He smiled at me. I think he likes me.

Lenore,

The boy's name is Christiano. His sister is Stephanie. Strange names, don't you think? I believe their parents were born in a different land and the children began their life somewhere else as well. Christiano is nice. I like him a lot. He is very protective of Stephanie, and won't let her out of his sight. Her eyes, enormous brown ones, are wide-open every time I see her, almost as if they are stuck that way and she cannot get them closed. I believe she has seen much terror—it lurks just behind the surface of those big eyes. She likes me. Today she took my hand as we gathered berries near the house. I had to make her let go so that I could pick the berries. She didn't understand. She looked sad. Later Christiano carried my pail, spilling berries from the top (I think he didn't want my pail to be fuller than his), and I picked Stephanie up and carried her back to the house. She was light as goose down. I let her eat some of my berries. She looked funny with bright red juice smeared all over her tiny face. She smiled at me, and then I thought she looked lovely.

I asked Christiano about his parents. He just clammed right up. His body was still there, but the rest of him left—just that fast. He walked along beside me, put the berries on the step beside mine, took Stephanie from my arms, and returned to Surice's house, all without a word or even a look in my direction. I can't be mad at him, because I think I would not want to talk about it if I were alone in a strange village with just my sister. Of course, I do not have any sisters. Still, I wonder...

Great King Immon, did you read my letter? I hope you have forgiven my harsh words about you. I did not really mean them. I just miss my life in the city. I miss the way things were before the Messenger came.

I don't miss the fire rituals. I don't miss the naked dancers who paraded through our streets, and I don't miss Chief Sodomon. I hate him. Please don't be mad at me for that—I don't mean to hate him, but I can't help it. He is really mean, and he is the reason we had to leave our old home where Miammi had her lovely garden and Miarrow went to work every day. We always celebrated when he came home with a bag of money, and we went to the market and bought fresh meat and vegetables and cakes. Miarrow says I will understand someday, but I doubt it.

Lenore,

Stephanie is ill today. Perhaps I should not have allowed her to eat so many berries. Her belly has been deprived much too long to tolerate that many after just a few days. Surice and Miammi are with her. Miarrow left just after Machato awoke. Miarrow travels though the jungle to seek the assistance of Pathalos, the physician who assisted Miarrow's mother at the time of his birth. Pathalos comes to visit after the children have been sent to their beds. There are not many women with child in the village, so I often wonder why he comes. He does not live in the jungle as we do, but walks the streets of the city freely, and comes by night with stealth and secrecy, like a thief. I wonder if Pathalos is the one who steals the children away in the night. No. For then they would be safe and Miarrow would not grieve. Pathalos is a kind man and brave, or he would not travel the perilous trails through the jungle night to come to us.

I wonder where babies live before they grow in their mothers' wombs. Perhaps they live, without bodies, in the presence of the Great King. The Messenger taught us that the spirit within us is a gift given by the Great King Immon, and that Immon never takes back that which he has given. I remember asking the Messenger, "Then what of the evil men who destroy the good and murder the innocent?" I did not like to think that they share the good gift with those of us who suffer the loss of our homes.

The Messenger held me on his lap with his arm around me. "Salina," he said rather sadly, "it is Immon's intention that all those who are born into the Kingdom of Adawm choose to follow Him into the Other Kingdom. But Immon is gracious, and will not violate the will of any person, even for his own good. Those who choose to yield their spirit to Dagog and follow him during the brief course of their time in the Kingdom of Adawm will share Dagog's eternal dwelling place in the darkness that lasts forever. It is, I assure you, a place of great suffering."

"Is there no hope then, for Sodomon and his followers who torment the Resisters even unto death?" I asked, secretly hoping my words were true.

"Always there is hope," he said. "As long as the breath of life is in a man, he may turn away from his allegiance to Dagog, and he will receive pardon and a Certificate of Redemption from Immon himself."

"Even if he lives all his years in the service of the Prince of the Darkness," I said, both amazed and a little angry, "he can change his mind at the last moment and share the Other Kingdom with those of us who forsake all to serve the Great King Immon—even from our youth?"

The Messenger smiled then and handed me to Miarrow. "You will not lose your reward, little one." He turned away, but not before I saw the tears in his eyes.

He left us then and went deeper into the woods. No one noticed that I followed him there, for Miarrow and Miammi were busy discussing his words between themselves. The Messenger knelt beside a rock and cried. It is sad to hear a grown man cry, Helgotha, for the tears seem to come from a different place than mine or even Miammi's. They seem to come from a river that forces its way through a man's chest and into his eyes, spilling over and splashing down like rain. At least that is how it was with the Messenger. I do not believe I have ever seen another man cry. When I thought of this, I became ashamed because I should not have seen his tears. He meant them to be private. I crept back to Miammi's side and buried my head in her skirts. She stroked my head, without interrupting the words she spoke to a young woman who sat, also with tears in her eyes, at Miammi's left hand. I believe I fell asleep, and Miarrow carried me to my bed.

That is why I love you, Helgotha, though you are very hard and cause me pain when I sit too long. The Messenger's tears were shed upon your back.

Do you think that I am silly, Helgotha? I don't think you do. I have been told that there was one who came to walk among the people in the Kingdom of Adawm, one so wonderful that even the rocks would have cried out his name had the people refused to. I have heard that the one who came was the Great King Immon himself, disguised as a citizen of the Kingdom of Adawm.

Would you have cried out, Helgotha? I know you would, but you won't have to, for I will do it for you.

It is difficult to balance my journal in my right hand and raise both hands toward the sky. Machato do you see me? Does the Great King Immon see me? Immon, King of the Other Kingdom, do you see me? Do you hear me as I shout, "Honor to Immon"? My voice is loud—I cry louder, "Honor to the Great King Immon!"

Miammi calls to me from the steps of our house. Even from this distance I can see her worried frown. There is much work to do today. I wave to her and finish writing. Helgotha, I hope you are happy—I just did your work for you.

Lenore,

Did you see the shadows in the forest yesterday? My heart is still pounding like the drums of war. As a matter of fact, I have heard the drums of war often lately. Shadows of strange beasts, drums sounding through the forest, why does no one speak of these things? Do I confuse reality with my imagination? No. This beast slinking between the trees is real. His eyes, orange with black slits in the middle, narrow when he looks at me. He sees me. Not only does he see me—I swear he knows me! I should not swear. I am sorry. I need to be really good for a while. The monster knows me, and he seeks me through the shadowed wood.

Lenore,

Another mystery. Bolati has gone on a journey, and Miammi will not tell me where he has gone. I am afraid that he seeks to kill the monster of the woods. Why else would he go when he is betrothed, except to protect his beloved princess.

Perhaps I am a little jealous. Bolati has little time for me since the stars began to shine through his eyes. He is lovesick. Disgusting.

I miss him. I miss Miarrow. I miss our home in the city with its lovely wooden fence. But I would not go back. I hate the festivals of pleasure and the smell of ashes that hangs over the city.

I will forget the things that I miss, just for today, and think only of the things that I enjoy.

I will never lose you, Machato, for you are with me always, though you do sometimes hide. You are as elusive (do you like that word, Lenore? It is in my lesson today) as the Great King Immon. Well, almost. You hide at night, but he hides always.

But he is always just as real as you are when you hide. I know because he reads words written on ashes.

Lenore,

It is late today, so I have only a short time to write. I slept late because sleep eluded me in the night. I stared at Machita's full roundness until my eyes hurt, but I could not fall asleep.

The shadowy beasts crept close to the village beneath the cover of night. There were many and they were all different, wolf-like beings, and creatures that resembled serpents but were not. I could tell by the way Machita glared at them, her stern glance bouncing off their slimy backs. Serpents are not slimy.

The worst were the manlike beings, all gray, stooped, and twisted, grinning with ugly teeth that glowed yellow in Machita's frowning light.

I do not fear wolves, serpents, or crocodiles. They do not wish to eat me, at least not if I avoid their hunting grounds. But these creatures seemed hungry and I have a feeling that they are hunting me.

Miarrow stands on the step. I must go.

Lenore,

It has been three days and I have seen no more shadowed beasts. Miammi says I have an overactive imagination. Perhaps she is right.

Miarrow is home at last. How I have missed him. He speaks of service to Immon. I wonder where Miarrow goes on his journey into the jungle, and what he does. Maybe someday I will follow him, if I am brave enough.

Lenore,

It is harvest and the crops have done well. Miarrow says that everyone is invited to join the elders at the council fire tonight. It will be a night of festivities, food, and games. I can hardly wait. Christiano and Stephanie will be there.

I have begun calling Stephanie little sister. She is only four years old and she follows me everywhere. I do not mind, except when I come here. I do not allow her to follow me to the writing stone. I refuse to share you, Helgotha, even with Stephanie. You are mine alone. You are always here for me, you never change, and you never complain when I sit on you. A true friend.

Miammi asked Christiano and me to go to the mushroom patch beneath the great mamboni trees on the west side of the river today, and gather enough for the stew she plans to cook for the festivities. I am a little afraid, but I will not tell Miammi. She will say that I have too much imagination. I suppose it will be all right if Christiano comes with me. He has grown and is now bigger and stronger than I am. I will stay near Christiano.

Lenore,

A terrible thing has happened. Little Stephanie has wandered away in the jungle. We have searched for her for days. It happened on the day I last wrote. I have been too busy and too heartsick to write since then.

Christiano and I took Stephanie with us to the mushroom patch. Stephanie had her own little pail, less than half the size of Christiano's and mine. She was humming as she skipped along. I recognized the tune, for Miammi used to sing it to me when I was only three or four.

Machato was high overhead, smiling down on us for all he was worth. I wished he would cover up with a few clouds for just a little while so that he would not burn the back of my neck with his kind attention. But he kept shining, and Christiano started chattering—how that boy can talk. I was listening and laughing, and then we looked around and Stephanie was gone. Just vanished.

I could have sworn that I saw strange forms flit between the trees, wicked things, but I didn't dare say it because Christiano was already so upset. I didn't want to make it worse for him.

We searched and called, but there was no answer. We found Stephanie's little pail on the ground, not far from where we had last seen her. Christiano started crying, not quietly, but deep, wrenching sobs that tore my heart out. I went to him and put my arms around him, and he hung on to me like I was his mother. Finally, we returned to the village and found Surice. The alarm went out, and a number of strong men, armed with sticks and rocks, went into the jungle and spread out to search for Stephanie.

It has been four days now, and there has been no sign of her. Demensi, who has grown old and is now allowed to sit with the elders at the fire, told me that a group of soldiers will try to go far beyond Sodomon's borders if that's what it takes to get her back. I wonder if that is where Miarrow has been going in the service of Immon. Perhaps that is why Miammi believes Miarrow is in danger.

Christiano wants to follow the soldiers. He wants me to come with him. I have not yet decided what I will do.

Lenore,

It is dark here, and damp. Christiano and I have been lost in the jungle for several days, I am not sure how many. The jungle didn't seem so frightening the day we left. We were only a few yards behind the soldiers, and it was great fun pretending to be soldiers ourselves, stalking the enemy, and crouching behind great rhododendrons to make ourselves invisible to Miarrow and the rest of them.

Machato was wide-awake then, beaming down on us from his perch above the clouds, making merry in the sky with scarlet macaws and blue malachites. As we walked, Christiano held my hand and began to tell me about his life in the City of Broken Dreams, the place of his parents' birth. He told me that his family followed one named Odair, who had left the city ahead of them, having been informed that there were other, better dreams for those who dared seek the Other Kingdom. I was glad to tell Christiano that I too had heard of the Other Kingdom and its ruler the Great King Immon. We fell behind the soldiers as we talked.

Machato sailed to new heights, and the metallic blue sky faded to powder blue, streaked with white clouds that were stretched so thin we could see through them. Suddenly, we realized that we were hungry. Each of us had brought a bag filled with food. I spread my blanket on the floor of the jungle and we sat there beneath the hole in the spreading green canopy and shared our simple fare. The food and the sunshine and the enjoyment of each other's company made us sleepy, so we lay down on the blanket in the fragrant mulch and slept. I don't know what we were thinking.

When we awoke, Machato had slipped off his perch and dropped out of sight behind the clouds. The soldiers' voices were silent and the jungle was waking up. Animals that feed at night began to stir, and insects with ferocious appetites buzzed around us.

Christiano gripped my hand tighter and we walked close together. My overactive imagination began to suggest serpents hiding under the leaves and hanging from the limbs overhead, orange eyes glowering from the shadows, and manlike creatures gliding behind trees, just out of sight. I did not know that imagination was contagious until Christiano started gasping at the precise moment I glimpsed the movement of the illusive creatures. It is a good thing that we found this old abandoned cabin when we did, because we were about to abandon our senses and run pell-mell through the jungle. We would probably have fallen into some deep ravine or animal lair—never to be seen again.

I thought of how Miarrow and Miammi would grieve, and a pleasant sadness filled my heart.

Lenore,

We have been three more days in the jungle since I last wrote. We ate the last of our food supply two days ago. The jungle is replete with berries and mushrooms, if one knows where to search and if one is not too squeamish, so Christiano and I have not gone hungry.

But we are feeling stalked. Miammi would say that my imagination is responsible, but I know better. Something, or someone, is hunting us. We look at each other when we hear a twig snap or an unfamiliar noise or rustling in the bushes. We don't say anything. But we know. We keep moving, hoping to catch up to the soldiers. We can see where they have been by the broken twigs and small articles cast aside, by footprints in the mulch, and the cold embers of their fires.

Machato is high overhead, casting diamond-clad fingers upon the small stream where we have found refreshment. Christiano sits upon a stone, his aching feet immersed in the cool water that bubbles up between the rocks. On his heels there are blisters the size of water beetles, and his toes are bloody from too-small shoes. I wish he had soft moccasins like mine. My feet do not hurt at all.

Christiano just laid his hand upon my arm. He has heard an unusual sound. I believe it is a voice. Someone is shouting. I have to go.

Lenore,

Today I hide behind the giant mamboni trees with Christiano, and hope that we will not be found. We have witnessed horrors beyond description—yes, beyond even my imagination—here in these woods.

Christiano huddles against me for comfort. Through my thin shirt I can feel his trembling. I apologize for my shaky writing, but I cannot hold my hands steady. We breathe with shallow breaths and do not dare whisper. As I write, Christiano watches, turning his head in all directions, listening with intensity that drains his face of color and tightens his lips. He looks much older than thirteen years as he reaches for my hand. There is a crashing in the brush...

Lenore,

I almost lost you five days ago. You fell from my hands when Christiano grabbed me, quite rudely, I thought, and pulled me into the low-growing cypress bushes. Throwing me to the ground, he dived in after me just as a monster, more horrible than anything Demensi ever described in my worst childhood memories, flew over our heads. I could not help staring at the beast through the spaces in the lacy limbs of the silvery bush. I wish I had not looked.

His form was like that of a bird, only much larger than any bird I have ever seen. He must have been at least a dozen feet across from the tip of one mammoth wing to the other. Compared to his body, his head was twice as large as I expected, with eyes like glass buttons, black and cold. I feared his beak. It looked to be razor sharp and was hooked on the end like a claw.

He opened his mouth as he flew, and the inside of that beak was lined with rows of sharp, pointy teeth. I could imagine what he would do to me if he had opportunity to clench my scrawny neck between those awful teeth and shake me as a dog shakes a garden snake.

One thing that saved us was the enormity of his wingspread. The trees are dense in that part of the woods, the canopy thick with overlapping branches bearing wide, green leaves and twisted vines that wrap themselves like serpents around trunks and branches, creating a netting that is difficult to penetrate from above.

Christiano thought we should keep moving, as the monster might have seen us. I dashed back to the tree and swooped you up into my arms, dear Lenore. I could not bear to lose you. Chris (it is too much bother to keep calling Christiano by his full name, which is much too long—the monster would be upon us before I could get the whole word out) thought I had lost my mind when he saw me running toward you, but I explained to him later that such a record holds much information that might give our enemy too much knowledge about us and our people. At that point, I believe he changed his mind and decided that I was very smart.

We traveled due west. I thought we would walk right into Machato's arms as he dropped beneath the treetops. Somehow he managed to elude us, and the night grew cold and dark without his friendly face to guide us. Machita did her best, but her light is faint compared to her brother's.

I stumbled often over twisted vines and rotten logs on the jungle floor. Once—I am ashamed to admit it—I did not get up immediately, but sat and cried like a little girl. Chris must have felt sorry for me because he turned away and pretended to look for wood to build a small fire. "A secret fire," he said. I was not sure it was wise, but I was too cold and miserable to care.

Lenore,

I awoke this morning with fickle Machato smiling into my face and Chris pressed tightly against my back. Both seemed very comforting after our ordeal, but I thought it would be immodest to linger in that position, so I pushed Chris, rather roughly, and said, "Get up, lazy boy, the day is half spent." Of course, it was not, but Chris rolled over and appeared embarrassed. I laughed at him and he shrugged. It is difficult to maintain our modesty in this wilderness.

I must go. Chris has that impatient look on his face again. It is no fun to walk through the jungle slapping at mosquitoes, fording crocodile-infested rivers, and dancing around serpents with an angry man at your side. Actually, we have not yet encountered crocodile-infested rivers, but I imagine it would not be fun.

Lenore,

There is a village in the valley below the hill where Chris and I have camped for the night. I see many fires, not just one, as we have in the heart of our village.

There are probably more people in this village than in ours, but we do not know if they are friendly. Chris wants me to stay on the hill while he sneaks through the forest to spy out the village. I say no! He lived in the city for eleven years. Two years in the jungle does not make him a better spy than I am. He thinks he has become a man already because in our land a boy becomes a man at twelve years of age, and usually takes a wife by fifteen. Chris appreciates this custom, because in the land of his birth a boy was not considered a man until at least eighteen. Perhaps his land does not afford such hardship as ours, and therefore childhood is not so easily displaced by the necessities of adult responsibility. Chris looks at me sternly, his lips compressed, and says, "Stay here and wait for me. I am the one who should go."

I do not disagree, but I smile because I know Chris will not awaken as early as I do. He does not know the morning face of Machato, for he has seldom seen it. While he sleeps, I will do what must be done.

Lenore,

I have returned from the village, but Chris is not to be found. Where could he have gone? There are no footprints in the mulch and no sign of distress. I am terribly worried, especially since I have discovered the secret of the village below. It is a terrible one. I cannot yet speak of it. Even to you.

Lenore,

Machato has deserted me, and Chris is still missing. I am alone, and the night is filled with strange and fearful sounds. I cannot turn back without Chris, and I cannot go into the village. I am lost and afraid. What shall I do, Lenore? Either way, I perish.

※

Lenore,

I am sitting on the ridge while the wind ruffles my hair and Machato smiles once more into my eyes. The rock beneath me reminds me of Helgotha; it is just as hard and uncompromising.

Chris returned just before Machita reached the top of the world last night. He will not speak of his experience. He offers no explanation, and I do not ask where he has been. His wide eyes and pale face tell me that he has buried what he has seen and heard deep inside, along with the other experiences that trouble his sleep.

"Do you know the secret of the village?" I asked him. He nods, and I know that I was not the only one who awakened early this morning.

※

Lenore,

I am weary of adventure, but peace and safety elude me. I sit in the shadows of a tall, spreading tree. Its limbs are rounder than I am and very long. It is covered with strange silver-green leaves that smell... comforting. I have packed my pockets full of them so that Miarrow and Miammi will believe that such trees exist. If I bring no proof, Miammi will think I only imagined it.

I am trying very hard to believe that I will one day see my village while I occupy my body. I am a Resister, and all Resisters know that our body is temporary, and will one day return to the soil, freeing our spirit—the part of us that dwells in the afterlife—to live unhindered in the Other Kingdom. I had hoped to occupy my fleshly vessel for many years, give myself to a man who shares my allegiance to the Great King Immon, and bear many children. My hopes mock me now.

Chris and I are in agreement that we must search the village that lies yonder in this fertile valley. It is a beautiful place, bordered on one side by the tall, fragrant trees and on another by the hill that rises to meet the ridge beyond the clouds. A river, clean and sweet, runs behind the thatched huts along the dirt road that divides the village into two equal parts.

It is a village of secrets. Every hut houses many children, and men bearing arms patrol the dirt road. A floating dock rides above the indigo water of the river, and two flatboats are tied there, one on either side of the pier.

The morning mist carries with it the sound of crying children, and I wonder, are Sashay and Stephanie among the children who wail for their mothers?

Lenore,

My heart weeps, I believe it has broken in my chest. Christiano asked me—no, he ordered me—to return home alone while he stays with the children at the village of secrets.

I watch from beneath a low-growing bush as Christiano approaches the armed man who guards the village. It is obvious that he does not patrol to protect the children in the huts, but to keep out impostors. Chris is an impostor, for he will know what they are doing here. He will pretend to be a lost child himself, but they will know that he is old enough to discern their secret.

He walks toward the guard. I am proud of him. He does not cower or cringe before the guard, who raises his weapon and shouts at him. Chris waves as he draws near, and then stands quietly while the guard approaches him and runs his hands over his body. Finding no weapon, the guard relaxes, but only a little. He motions Chris toward the first hut in the row, then enters behind him.

"I should have forced you to let me go with you, Christiano," I whisper. But in my heart I know better. Who will lead the soldiers to the secret village if neither of us returns? Who will save the children?

I am lonely but no longer afraid. I have decided that, like Miarrow, I am a soldier of the Great King Immon. A soldier must be brave. A soldier must know how to find her way home. And I will do both.

Lenore,

It has been six months since Christiano went into the secret village. If only we had known, the village was no more than two days' distance from our home.

There was rejoicing when I stumbled into our village, even though I must have been a very unpleasant sight. My clothing was filthy and torn, my body covered with scratches and abrasions. My hair was tangled with a thousand cockleburs, and my face a mass of mosquito bites. It is a wonder that I did not get the jungle fever. No one can quite understand why I did not. But I know.

The next morning, sleepy rays of rosy-gray light swarmed through the lacy foliage to kiss the jungle floor. A dozen soldiers were gathered at the fire, brewing coffee over the open flame. As soon as Machato roused from his slumber, they left, walking wordlessly two by two along the narrow pathway through the jungle. My heart went with them. My directions were more accurate than I supposed, and they soon found the secret village. It was abandoned. There was no sign of the children and no sign of Christiano. At least there were no dead bodies and no fresh graves. Christiano lives. I know that he does, and one day I will see him again. There are those who say that I hope for the impossible. I say to them, "You do not know, but I know." I always know.

Lenore,

Bolati is home. He returned in my absence, but the old Bolati will never return. He is different. His face is scarred, and he walks with a dreadful limp. His left ankle is twisted, and he leans on a stick to help him along. Miammi says his beloved was happy to see him, scars and all. She does not leave his side, and the stars still shine in her eyes when she looks at him. They are now husband and wife. When Bolati's eyes find hers, his poor, sad face lights up like a sunbeam thrust through an angry cloud, so I suppose I can forgive her for taking him away from me.

Resisters

CHAPTER 3: AGE TWELVE

Lenore,

It is my twelfth birthday. I am a woman today. It is strange, perhaps, but I do not feel any different. I felt like a woman when I was eleven. Not when I was ten, but at eleven everything changed.

I am going through the rite of passage at a feast tonight. Everyone knows that. Four other girls will be honored as well. But only Miarrow and Miammi know about the other ceremony. Only they are allowed to know that a daughter of the village has become a soldier in the army of the Great King Immon. I must go. It is time.

Lenore,

Last night my life changed forever, for I learned that Miarrow, my own father, is a general in the army of the Great King Immon.

I will never forget the tears in his eyes as he commissioned me for service, and I will never forget his words. I write them here so that not one of them will ever perish from my memory.

"Most do not understand our warfare. They believe that all battles must be waged with the sword. They believe that the object of warfare is to overcome the enemy, and that the bad people should die so the good can live. This may be a necessary evil in the Kingdom of Adawm, where oppression must be met with violent resistance, and destruction of the body determines the outcome.

"In the Other Kingdom it is not so, for the battle is not against flesh and blood, but against the powers of darkness under the dominion of Dagog, the Prince of the Darkness. It is a battle of the invisible body—the spirit within the fleshly vessel—against the powers of darkness that would destroy not only the fleshly vessel in which we live, but the invisible body that has been created to live forever.

"If you, Salina, join the army of the Great King Immon, you must be willing to lose your life in the Kingdom of Adawm in order to gain never-ending life in the Other Kingdom. Your highest purpose will be to live not for yourself but for others, to sacrifice yourself, if necessary, for a greater good. The armies of the Great King are instruments not of death, but of life.

"Salina, are you ready to lay down your life at the feet of your enemy, if need be, so that your enemy may look into the Other Kingdom through your eyes?"

"I am."

"Salina, are you ready to do good to those who hate you, and rescue those who have been taken captive by Dagog, the Prince of the Darkness, as much as you are able, at any price?"

"I am."

"Then I commission you for service in the army of the Great King Immon, to follow in the footsteps of the one who has faithfully performed everything that you have promised to do, and set the example by giving up his own life at the hands of his enemies."

I am glad that I was kneeling when, as Miarrow pronounced these last words, he touched my forehead with oil from a small crystal vial, for I fear, had I been standing, my knees would have buckled, and I might have embarrassed myself and Miarrow by fainting dead away.

I may not be able to write for a while, Lenore, for I believe that from this day forward I will be very busy in the service of the Great King Immon.

Lenore,

We are well hidden in our home here in the jungle, surrounded by the deep woods on three sides, with the Roan River behind us. Resisters in other villages do not fare so well. We have relocated families and even entire villages many times, and still Sodomon rages against us. The fires offered to the gods blaze red with the blood of Resisters.

I write by the light of my candle, for at first light I join Miarrow and ten other soldiers in a rescue. For the first time, I have been told why the children come to Surice's house. I grieve for the parents who have been slain and for the orphans who survive them. Christiano, how brave you are, an orphan who offered your life to save other orphans. You knew better than I the agony of the children in the secret village, wailing for parents who would never again come to comfort them. I hope you live, Christiano, and I hope to see you again. I will not forget you, and I will not forget Stephanie and Sashay. I will not forget the children of the secret village. Someday, I will find you.

Lenore,

Surice has asked that I apply for a position as administrative assistant to Chief Sodomon. He says that my ability to articulate, and my intuitive understanding of espionage, would greatly advance our cause among the captives of Dagog. I do not relish living in the Land of Lasciviousness. I will be as out of place as a third hand, useful perhaps, but definitely an abnormality. Does the Great King Immon truly ask this of me, or is this the whim of a desperate old man?

Lenore,

It has been more than a week since I last wrote. I have missed you. How quickly opportunities unfold when it is the will of the Great King. Not always—for it is the will of Immon that Christiano be found, but it has been a year since I last saw him, and I have received no word of him. Does he yet live? Perhaps I will learn the answer in my new position.

Yes, I am now administrative assistant to the chief. I live in a beautiful home, a tent, actually, but one such as you never saw. The walls are stretched leather, stained on the outside with the brown fruit of the walnut tree, and bleached to pale beige on the inside. Braided rugs adorn the dirt floor and the walls.

My tent is within five feet of the chief's, and I often hear his voice raised as he argues with the council. I see already that all is not well between Chief Sodomon and those who sit at his fire. I miss Miarrow and Miammi. I miss Christiano.

Lenore,

I saw the monster again today. He was in the marketplace with a mob of disorderly soldiers. They were interrogating an old woman. He couldn't have recognized me. I look just like everyone else who lives here—short skirt and low-cut blouse. It is the "uniform" of my present occupation. I hate it, but Surice assures me that Immon will not hold my immodesty against me. My straight, black hair has been cut to shoulder length, and I am wearing bangs. I do look awful. Even Christiano would not recognize me.

It seems the monster can change shapes. He looked very much like a man today, attired to fit the position of counselor to Chief Sodomon. He claims to carry out the orders of the chief, but it seems to me that he is the one giving them, putting words in the old chief's mouth while he stares at him with those glassy black eyes, like a dog trifling with a rabbit. His sharp beak of a nose is so much like that of the monster in the forest that I expect it to have two rows of tiny, pointed teeth inside.

My associates think he is quite handsome. They think he is witty. I think wily would better describe the creature. He preys upon the younger girls, especially the pretty ones.

The chief gave me a sheaf of papers to go through today. I am afraid to read them. I can already guess what I will find.

Lenore,

I have done a frightful thing. If I am found out, my ashes will ascend to the throne of the Great King Immon by morning. I do not fear this, for I have pledged my life for the cause, but I have only begun to realize what is done to Resisters who are caught in unlawful acts. I ask only for a quick death.

Lenore,

The thing is done, and I am safe, at least for the moment. I have sent word to Miarrow along with the escort and the child. My heart is broken for the parents whom I could not save, and for the child orphaned by the evil monster who moves the minds and numbs the hearts of the rulers of this land.

As for Assad, I would kill him with my own hands if that were possible, but that is a job best left to the Great King himself. In due time, he will avenge his children.

Lenore,

I am sorry I have not written in three months. Unspeakable sorrows have paralyzed my hand and my heart—and I am a part of the ugliness of all this, the bloodshed and the slaughter. It is my hand that signs the certificate that saves some and sends others to the fire. My only consolation is this: if a servant of Dagog served in this position, none would be saved. I tell myself that it is not I who send the innocent to their deaths, but Chief Sodomon and those who influence him. If this is proper reasoning, then it is not Chief Sodomon and his peers, but Dagog, the ruthless Prince of the Darkness, who rules over them, who is responsible.

Christiano, you would not like me now. I do not like me either, but until I am released from this dire duty, probably by death, I will do what I must.

Today I altered the certificate that condemned a family of five, changing the 5 to a 3. It was not too difficult to disguise, but the rescue was tedious to arrange. It was necessary to first ascertain whether the accusers would be present to gloat over their victims. My sources say that the accusers live a great distance from the city, and will not be present at the fire. The family was arrested on their farm and delivered by the constable to the council. It is unlikely that anyone else will know that there are five family members and not three as the certificate now reads. The executioner will call for three. The parents and an infant will be surrendered to him. They will perish in the fire.

The other two children have been moved to a place of safety. If they are discovered now, we will all perish. In two hours Machita will rise to her throne among the clouds and shine her pale light upon the path that leads to my village. There is no time to inform Miarrow. I will have to escort the children myself.

It will be a challenge to travel to the village in the darkness and deliver the children to Surice's house, then return to my tent before prying eyes are opened beneath Machato's rude stare. Already my head feels like the bowl the chef uses to grind the corn—pounding it with the stone pestle until the kernels are crushed into fine powder.

The children are hidden in the jungle not far from the city. They are old enough to understand, somewhat, the peril of their position. They do not yet know their parents' fate. We dare not tell them until they are safely delivered to the house of Surice. Experience has taught us that their reaction to grief, while unpredictable, could expose both the children and us to the executioner. I must go and find them. Machita has ceased to climb.

I stuff my ears with cotton to stifle the sound of screams pouring from the fire. They will not last long, but I will hear them in my dreams long after they are silenced.

Lenore,

Just after midnight, Miarrow met me in the woods near our village. He is tired. His smile barely reached his brown eyes, and I miss the twinkle that used to leap out at me when he looked at me. He brought me a fresh loaf of bread that Miammi baked this morning. Her lovely hands never forget her only daughter.

Miarrow asks how I am. I lie and say that I am fine. Another mark against me,

O Great King, if you are keeping score. Miarrow stares into my eyes, which are lighter than his. And he knows. He squeezes my shoulder and says, "Carry on, soldier." I grab him and hug him so tightly that he can't speak and I can't breathe. When I let him go, I turn and race back through the jungle. Time grows short.

CHAPTER 4: AGE THIRTEEN

Lenore,

It is my thirteenth birthday. No one will celebrate, for I must spend the day in the Land of Lasciviousness, and no one here must know that I am only thirteen. Though I am small, I look and speak well beyond my years. If this is a gift, I offer it to the service of the Great King Immon.

I am growing old in the Land of Lasciviousness. I long to yield to the numbness that seems to cloak the citizens as a garment. The city streets are congested with people who hug their children, laugh at each other's jokes, and kiss their wives, even while passing the fire and smelling the stench of burning flesh from last night's sacrifice. Insanity dwells within the borders of this city. I pray that I do not become a part of it. I drink at the same well as everyone else, but the water cannot contaminate the spirit that has been surrendered to the Great King. At least, that is my hope.

|||| |||| |||

Lenore,

I am grateful for a good day. No one has been fed to the fire for more than a week. Sodomon's secret police must be on a holiday.

I am having a party. Can you believe it? I have invited all the girls from Sodomon's hall to come. I did not invite the dancers. I could not bear to do it. I know they are bound to the Prince of the Darkness, enslaved by his seduction and deception. I know they are in jeopardy of losing the Other Kingdom altogether, but I cannot invite them. I should want to save them, but I do not. I watch them dance around captive men, women, and children, wailing out their chants to the god of the night, delighting in their service to Dagog, and I hate them. Another mark against me, but I cannot help it.

Lenore,

You will not believe what happened. Sonora, my personal secretary, came to the party. She was sad and said little. After everyone else left to go home, she stayed behind and asked me the secret of my confidence. I did not tell her of my service to the Great King Immon. I am not so foolish as that, but I invited her to come back next week and have dinner with me.

One of the girls, DeMaile, brought her friend Nasha. DeMaile said that Nasha is especially kind to others but has few friends. I will befriend her. Perhaps she will become a sympathizer. There are possibilities here. Finally, I believe that I am beginning to make some progress.

Lenore,

Today I am at home in my village. I will return to the city in three days, but it is good to be with Miarrow and Miammi and my brothers. Bolati and Demensi look at me with new eyes. I believe I have earned their respect.

Bolati has surprised me by producing a brand-new niece to take my mind off my troubles. Little Samia is a perfectly formed doll baby. Until now, I have not been envious of other girls my age who have married and borne children. Now I envy them! Why could I not be as they are—content to bake bread in the stone ovens and lie beside a man of my own choosing?

In my heart of hearts, I know that the only man I will ever love said goodbye to me in the village of secrets. Having babies with any other would be both tedious and cruel. No. I will continue to work to save other people's children for as long as King Immon grants me opportunity to do so.

I look around and see many children here. Some of them are alive because of my efforts. They laugh and play with the other children. They have been adopted by loving families who serve Immon by taking care of orphans left behind by those who refused to bow to Dagog. Perhaps, O Great King, that is counted in my score. Perhaps there is hope for me yet.

~~HH~~ ~~HH~~ III

Lenore,

Much has changed in the past two years, but Helgotha remains exactly the same. This is something that I can count on.

Machato, you kiss my face as if you loved me still, but I know that you also kiss the faces of those who would throw me into the fire as easily as they would a broken twig. You are a fickle friend.

The air is heavy with the fragrance of orchids today, their blossoms twine among the green vines that grasp the trees and open to the sky. The straw roofs of our huts are buried beneath crushed blooms tossed from the hands of women and children who, even in poverty, like things that are pretty and that smell good.

Beneath my feet the grass feels like velvet, the fabric of kings. Helgotha will cause no more discomfort to my lower extremities today, for I will lie on the soft green carpet and breathe the mixed fragrance of grass and blossom, fresh air and home. Especially fresh air. I have forgotten the smell of air unencumbered by the odor of burnt human flesh.

Lenore,

It is my last day in paradise. Or so it seems to me. The happiness and hearth of home make up for the lost grandeur of kings' palaces and tents fashioned of exquisite leather and fabrics.

I will say goodbye to Miarrow and Miammi. I will hug my brothers and hold little Samia one last time. Who knows what tomorrow may bring? I will cherish

|||| |||| |||

these last moments at home and allow no sadness to diminish my joy.

Lenore,

I am happy today. Not in every part of my heart, but in enough of it that I can smile back at Machato and, like other women my age, swing my hips when I walk through the marketplace. I notice the interested glances of the young men, but I do not return them.

I will not be alone today. Nasha is coming to the market with me. Did I tell you about Nasha? She is tiny, like the meadow finch, and quick, with big almond-colored eyes that are flecked with chocolate. Her olive skin is flawless, and her cheeks would be coral even if she did not pinch them to make them so. She will be thirteen next week, and I plan to buy her a gift, though she does not know it.

I will write more by candlelight tonight.

Lenore,

It was a wonderful day. Sodomon pays me well, and I have saved a little for gifts. I bought a tiny baby doll for Samia. It is soft and cuddly and has yellow yarn for hair.

I learned much about Nasha today as we sat in the teashop together and sipped strong black tea. Nasha likes hers with sugar, but I do not. Little sugar was available when I learned to drink hot beverages.

I understand the sadness in Nasha's eyes more today. Her father is a general under Assad's command. I have seen the scars on her body, but I know that there are more of them where scars are veiled to the eyes of flesh. I see the reflection of such scars in her wide eyes as she opens the door to her heart and takes out childhood memories that sadden me. She holds little back. Perhaps she has few friends who have ears as good as mine.

I bought her a journal. It is small, with only a few pages, and has bright red covers. It is not nearly as nice as you, Lenore, and I told her that she may call her journal by any name other than Lenore. You see, I am not fickle like our friend Machato.

Nasha likes to walk beneath the morning face of Machato, as I do, and she lives in the communal circle near Sodomon's tent as well. We will take our morning walks together. There is much that I would like to know about this tiny birdlike girl who seems ready to fly away should any get too close.

CHAPTER 5: AGE FOURTEEN

Lenore,

I am fourteen today.

Lenore,

Chief Sodomon has asked that I come to his house just after Machato drops behind the trees. The skies are aflame with celestial fire amid powder blue space and white bubbles of cloud. I stare long into the heavens, admiring Machato's farewell to the day, and wondering if I will see his face tomorrow.

Lenore,

It is late, and I write by the light of a single candle. I have just returned from Sodomon's house. My hands shake and I find breathing difficult. I must calm down and clear my thinking.

Sodomon has discovered our village. After nearly three years of unsuccessful searching, one of his allies stumbled upon it yesterday. A massive attack is to be made tomorrow. Tomorrow, Lenore!

Does Sodomon suspect that I come from the village on the eastern ridge by the Roan River? Why would he give me this information when my village is the one he plots to attack? He has never given me information on impending attacks before. Mere coincidence? I don't think so.

I will warn my people. If I die... I die.

Lenore,

It is early morning. Machita hid her face last night among the gray darkness of the clouds. This was good for me. I slipped out of my tent shortly after meeting with Sodomon, knowing that I should wait, but having no heart to do so.

I was out of breath and covered in sweat when I reached the village. I ran straight to Surice's house and banged on his hut. He must have heard my steps before I ran up on his porch, because he was at the door almost before I knocked. He pulled me inside. "What is wrong, child?" He asked me. Between panting breaths, I spewed the awful truth into his ears. Immediately, he ran outside and began sounding the alarm, clanging the heavy metal ball against a steel rod with all his might. Men, and some women, poured out of the houses and stood open-mouthed, staring at Surice and at me there beside him.

When Surice had quieted everyone, he told them, in a calm voice that amazed me, that Sodomon's forces would be upon them in about four hours, and advised them to prepare to execute the plan of escape.

I know the plan. I am reasonably sure that my people escaped without harm, though they have surely lost all of their belongings and the food that has been carefully stored up for the winter.

I am ready to go to the hall, though I am not due to arrive there for a full hour. I have paid special attention to my attire and grooming. It will not do for me to appear troubled or fatigued. I am ready to put a smile on my face and march into the hall as if, for all the world, I love working in Sodomon's death camp.

Lenore,

I am tired this morning. It has been a week since my people evacuated our village, and I have received a message that all is well with them. Miarrow is away on a mission for the Great King Immon. I have heard that he has discovered another secret village. It is populated with armed guards and dozens of small children. He and his command of ten men watched from behind the great mamboni trees as the guards emptied the huts, forcing the children onto flat-bottom boats.

I want to be there—to be present when our forces intercept the boats and free the children. I have no doubt about their fate if Miarrow is unsuccessful. The slave market bulges with orphaned and abandoned children. They are sold for the price of a pig or a lamb in the market, and treated worse than the dogs that roam the city streets.

If Immon wills, Miarrow, perhaps you will discover news of Christiano. I hope you capture the armed guards and make those sorry sons of perdition talk! I am sorry, Great King Immon, if my words offend you, but I have seen such guards before. I know I should hope to rescue even such vermin as these from the power of the Prince of the Darkness, but my heart is rebellious today, and I hope that they perish in the clawed hand of the master whom they serve with such delight. Forgive me, O Great King. I am an unworthy servant.

Lenore,

Once again I have seen the monster that Christiano and I encountered in the forest, the beast of prey that flew above us, the beast with the glassy black eyes and sharp hooked beak. I saw him today in the tent of Sodomon. He knew me, Lenore. I am sure of it.

I must lay down my pen and quiet myself before I can continue in a legible hand.

Dear Lenore, I must tell you about the beast. He sat before the fire in Sodomon's tent, his hands folded as if in prayer. But he was not praying. He was thinking. He turned his eyes on me and I nearly fainted.

Then Sodomon said, "My dear Salina, I would like to introduce you to my associate, Assad."

I wanted to drop through the floor, to disappear. Those glassy eyes seemed to penetrate my mind and read my thoughts. I tried to think of Machato and Machita and Helgotha. I refused to think the names of my family and my people. Some say Dagog cannot read our thoughts, and I hope this is true, but I dared not take the chance. I managed to say, "Glad to meet you, sir." I hoped that Immon would not hold the lie against me.

Lenore,

Winter is upon us, bringing a deluge of rain and a fresh crop of biting insects. My people have lodged in a ravine near the river. It is well hidden, but infested with mosquitoes, snakes, and other vermin. Some of my people are not well. All are suffering.

I managed to procure a large shipment of food early this week, and Miarrow sent his troop to take it home. We maintain communication almost daily now, via runners who risk jungle fever to meet with me in the crowded marketplace.

I have learned that much of the evil we blame on Sodomon is not his doing after all, but that of his chief counselor Assad. I am convinced that Assad is none other than Dagog himself.

Assad, who was once a spy in the camp of the Resisters, knows the truth, but he despises it. The truth is his enemy; therefore he hates all those who love the truth. He controls Sodomon, and forces him to perform his will. It is not that Sodomon is a good man, but his cruelty has been tempered by time and his heart softened by the blood of Resisters. He dares not defy Assad because Assad is more powerful than he. When Assad can no longer control Sodomon, he will overthrow him.

Lenore,

Sodomon called me to his tent again. I no longer fear him. I have an uneasy feeling that he knows I serve Immon, but he does not say it. Today, he asked me if I believe there is an afterlife.

I answered yes.

Without surprise, he asked if I believe that one who has lived a life of wickedness can do anything to achieve it.

I answered no. One cannot achieve that which has already been accomplished for him by another.

He asked no more, but dismissed me with a wave of his hand. I left him there, sitting before his fire, hunched into a heavy blanket, staring at the flames.

Lenore,

Surice will lead my people back to the Land of Lasciviousness today. I fear he is leading them to their doom. I will die with them.

Lenore,

The incessant rains of winter are behind us. Machato has repented of abandoning us and makes amends by pouring buckets of golden sunshine upon us every day. You are forgiven, Machato. You may lessen your labor and allow us to have clouds for a day. The crops are wilting in the field.

I am in the marketplace today, shopping for Sodomon. He trusts no one else. I should be honored, but I am annoyed. He allows Assad to bully him like a little boy who has no father. I sit in a sequestered booth, drinking tea after a long day at work. My feet hurt. How I miss my moccasins and mulched paths. I was not born to be a city woman.

Oh, no! Here comes trouble. Three men and two women have been sitting quietly at a table nearby, drinking their tea and talking in low voices. Assad's death squad is approaching them. Dear Immon, King over all that is and was and ever will be, send your warriors to the defense of these innocents. I see murder in the eyes of Assad's henchmen. They talk among themselves. I must do something

Lenore,

Trouble averted often breeds more trouble. So it is. I knocked over the table of Immon's servants, getting their attention rather abruptly, and mouthed the words "Look behind you." One of them glanced back, saw the trouble coming, and promptly drew his wife and the others to their feet. I apologized profusely, making sure that Assad's henchmen recognized me. They are not bold enough to attack an official on Sodomon's staff—not yet.

But they noted me. They will watch me hereafter. I must be careful or I will be fed to the fire, and there will be nothing that Sodomon can do to stop it.

Lenore,

The net draws tighter. I met with Surice today. He informed me that there has been rioting in the streets, protests against the Resisters living in the city. One banner read: If you are not with us you are against us. Another: Your intolerance will not be tolerated. Oneida is punishable by death. And the worst: Offended by me and my ways? That's all right—your body is free fuel.

Oneida, Lenore! We stand convicted, all of us, of The one crime that demands the penalty of death in the Land of Lasciviousness. We have broken the ancient law. Well do I remember it:

> *All should live uncensored*
> *by a public-minded view.*
> *Whatever is right in your own eyes*
> *is the righteous thing to do.*

To disagree with the law is to commit Oneida. And to agree with the law is to enter into a lie and bind ourselves again to the Prince of the Darkness. Therefore, we resist!

There is talk of depriving Resisters of their children. Assad has told the populace that raising children who believe in the Great King Immon is an endangerment to the ways of the Land of Lasciviousness, and therefore all Resisters should be required to register—so that their children can be taken from them and raised by those who honor the Prince of the Darkness.

Lenore,

Assad has convinced Sodomon that the riots are the fault of the Resisters, though they have done nothing, not even defend themselves. Sodomon knows better. I know that he does. He has become helpless.

Someone is at my door...

This is the worst day of my life. My dear Miarrow has fallen beneath the sword of Assad's assassins. Miammi has just left, leaning on the arm of Bolati. She droops like a wilted flower. I never realized she was so small, so fragile.

Bolati says the streets run red with the blood of Resisters. He has taken his family to a safe house deep in the jungle. I wonder if there is such a thing as a safe place within the Kingdom of Adawm for the children of Immon.

Lenore,

Assad has twisted Sodomon's arm yet again. Sodomon has decreed that all who refuse to dance in honor of the Prince of the Darkness will be fed to the fire as an offering, to appease the anger of the Prince who rules over this land. A death sentence hangs over the head of every Resister. Dagog believes, once again, that he has won. It is not the first time he has shown his ignorance. When he initiated the death of the Great King Immon in the Valley of E'ure, he celebrated his victory—a shallow one that proved to be his undoing. He does not yet know it, because he is vain and ignorant concerning such matters. He piles up judgment unto himself and his followers. I pity the beast. After he has robbed us of our fleshly vessels, there is no more that he can do, for we are forever in the service of our Great King, rejoicing in the halls of the Other Kingdom. Happy. Whole. Together with those we love. And Dagog is undone.

Lenore,

I could not maintain my position in this evil land were it not for Nasha. Each day we walk beneath the towering trees in the cool of the evening, when gentle breezes stir the leaves overhead and blue malachites dart among the branches, their short, rounded wings whirring in a shimmering blur.

Today Nasha asked, 'Do you know any Resisters, Salina?' Not an unusual question, since we were passing a group of oddly quiet men and women who watched with careful eyes as we passed.

"Perhaps," I answered. Also careful.

"What are they like?"

"Those that may be Resisters—and remember I said 'may be'—are no different from you and me. In some ways, we are all Resisters."

Nasha seemed startled. "What do you mean?"

"Some resist the ordinances that require them to honor a prince whom they have no wish to serve and who is not the ordained ruler of the land. According to law, Sodomon is chief—not the gods or prince or whatever you choose to call them. Others resist the king of the Other Kingdom, saying he has no right to rule over them, and doubting his existence because he does not show his face in this land. All resist something—the difference lies only in what we choose to resist."

Nasha was quiet—thinking. She seemed solemn when she said goodnight and turned to walk back to her tent.

⸘

Miarrow, I miss you. My heart weeps a river every night, and my eyes are red by morning. No one notices, for many eyes weep in this land, and those who do not weep tarry long at the wine, and have red eyes just like the rest of us.

Lenore,

The darkness is thicker than wine tonight, the moon red as blood. The voices of the Resisters cry out from the ground.

I hear Sodomon, fretting in his sleep inside his tent, which stands within the shadow of my own. Other sounds, dark and ominous, seep between the seams of his royal leather walls; beastly sounds, unnatural, but bearing resemblance to the growling of a wolf lusting after prey, the hissing of serpents, and the low whine of near-human voices, not alive, but not quite dead. Miammi would no longer say that I imagine such sounds, for she has heard them in the streets of this land, and she refuses to step outside her door unless Bolati or Demensi is with her.

I cover my ears with my hands, and squeeze my eyes shut against the shadows that pace outside my door, translucent forms that slink and lurk, eyes that gleam through the crimson haze.

The crier in the street calls, "Peace, peace," but there is no peace.

Lenore,

I cannot stay here. Death parades in the streets by day, and evil is palpable in the still darkness of the night. Tortured voices and unnatural cries awaken me, if I dare to sleep, throughout the night. Today I will tell Sodomon that I am returning to the house of Miarrow. I will beg to be excused so that I can properly grieve my father and care for my mother.

I will not deny my allegiance to the Great King Immon, but I am wasted for his service. I must go home.

Lenore,

The sadness in Chief Sodomon's eyes haunts me. He merely nodded when I asked to be released. There was despair in his silence.

Miammi and my brothers have joined other Resisters on the east side of the Roan River. They are depending on the crocodile-infested waters to protect them from sudden attack. It is a good strategy as long as they do not need to cross the river themselves. The shallows are composed of waist-deep muck beneath the willowy grass, and it is difficult to distinguish the fallen logs from the rigid backs of the crocodiles that wallow in the muck, waiting for their dinner.

I will join the Resisters at the river's edge tomorrow.

Machita

CHAPTER 6: AGE FIFTEEN

Lenore,

I am sorry that I have not written since coming home. I am trying to forget, at least for a while, the sorrow of Sodomon's house.

Today is my fifteenth birthday. In my country a woman expects to be married, or at least betrothed, by the age of fourteen. I confess I did not expect to be alive at fifteen. Since I have made it this far, perhaps I will see sixteen as well.

It is good to be home, though home is seldom located in one place for very long. Our survival depends on being able to move quickly when threatened, and on always having a place prepared to receive us at a moment's notice.

I have found a stone almost as tall as Helgotha and broader, which is good, for I am not as thin as I was at eleven. I no longer name the stones as I did then, though it is difficult to think of the sun by any name other than Machato. He is still my very fine and fickle friend.

I miss Nasha and our morning walks. Machato, do you smile on Nasha, walking alone in the Land of Lasciviousness this morning, even as you beam your affection on my head as I sit upon a nameless stone in my hidden village?

There is activity at the river's edge. A messenger has come. I must go.

Lenore,

I rose before the light of morning today, while Machita still reigned over the night, bidding her beloved brother to be patient. I rejoice that Nasha, my dear friend, has come to our hidden village. She comes in the company of Demensi, who seems quite smitten with her. Who can blame him?

Nasha slept on a mat in the house of Miammi, sharing my corner for the night. Her dreams were troubled. She cried out often, and reached her hands as if grasping at some invisible form. Her pillow was wet with tears long before I rose to seek solitude and write my troubled thoughts.

Lenore,

Nasha has become the sister I never had. Her face has begun to lose its sadness— most of the time. We have become a team, helping with the orphans as they arrive, and baking bread in the stone ovens for families who have taken in more mouths than they can feed.

In the morning, I need solitude and Nasha needs sleep. Like Christiano, she does not like the morning face of Machato. I seek my writing stone and she seeks peace in slumber, but she seldom finds it. Her dreams are troubled.

Lenore,

There is a tiny tattoo on Nasha's shoulder. I have never seen it before because her clothing covers it, but she was forced to borrow one of my sleeping shirts, for all of her clothes fell into the river as Demensi brought her across. The crocodiles were swift to tear into the cotton bag and drag it off before Demensi could recover it.

The tattoo is in the shape of a sliver of moon riding above a single star. This is the sign of the fire dancers.

A fire rages in my heart, a secret fire that none can see except perhaps the Great King Immon who, from his throne in the Other Kingdom, sees and knows all. The fire will devour, as fire is intended to do, but I know that I will decide the fodder that fuels it. What will I feed to the fire—my hatred or my love? I love Nasha as a sister, as the friend who walks with me beneath the smiling face of Machato and lifts my weary heart. I hate Nasha, the fire dancer who laughs when children and their parents scream, and treads upon the faces of the meek. For I know what fire dancers do. I watched them—once—and wished, secretly, that the flames would consume them, let them scream in pain and fear, let their flesh melt from their bones...

I am lost in my pain, Machato. I do not want to see Nasha's face this morning. I do not want to see Nasha until I know which flame I will choose to feed.

Lenore,

I should not have returned to the city. Assad has marked me. Trouble is bound to come of it.

Lenore,

I am burning. The heat of the fires of death rage outside the cell where I have been confined. I cover my ears, but still I hear the screams of the innocent who die in the fire. The guards poke and prod at those who are condemned. They have herded them like cattle inside the barbed-wire fence that surrounds the shallow pit where a perpetual fire burns against the sky.

My ankles are shackled. Footsteps approach.

Lenore,

It is safe now to take you from your hiding place beneath my skirts. Miammi was right to sew pockets into my underskirt. I must tell her... if ever I see her again.

Sodomon was here. He stood outside my door, gazing through the bars on the small window, helpless sadness on his face. It is not by his order that I am here. I know that it is not.

His small gift means much to me. About half an inch long and soft as a bunny's ear, I hold them in my hands—a pair of earplugs to help me shut out the horror that I cannot ignore. Wait. There is something inside. A tiny piece of paper on which the words "Do not despair" are written in tiny print. What does Sodomon know? Are the soldiers of my king aware of my arrest? Do they plan a rescue?

Miarrow, how I miss you. If only I could see you now, talk with you, be comforted with my head against your chest. Perhaps I will see you soon, maybe even tonight, though I think they have other plans for me. I will be brave, Miarrow. I will not deny my king.

Lenore,

I am sorry for the blood that has soaked into the page as I write. I am not badly injured, for they are not yet ready to offer my body to their gods. First they interrogate me.

I know their strategy. They will use threats to manipulate me by fear. This they have begun, teasing me with sharp instruments designed to fill my mind with the awful possibilities that my torture may provide for the executioner's amusement. If fear fails to break me—as it will—they will use the torture devices. I refuse to imagine what that will be like.

I am very tired, Lenore. I will use the earplugs and my imagination. I will go far away and find Christiano. Imagine his joy when he sees me again. Perhaps he is already with Miarrow in the Other Kingdom. I hope I may be there also—soon.

Lenore,

They have given up on me. They did not torture me much. Someone either bribed the executioner or blackmailed him. He looked at me with hateful eyes, but he has signed my death warrant without the usual preliminaries. For this I am grateful.

I will go to the fire tonight. I have no way to get you into safe hands, my friend, and so we go together. With you hiding beneath my skirts. Coward. I thought better of you.

My dear Lenore, it is said that you can take nothing with you from the Kingdom of Adawm when you cross the Crystal River. I will petition my king, the Great Immon, to make one exception. If he has been keeping score of my shortcomings, it may test his generosity to allow me to enter his kingdom, even without my precious journal. But I no longer believe that he does this; it is not his way. He is as a father with his child as far as we are concerned, and Miarrow forgot—always—my misbehaviors, remembering only the things that honored me.

Lenore,

You thought that you would have become ashes by now, did you not? I as well. It seems we have a reprieve. Just after Machato sank beneath the trees, igniting the fires of heaven, Sodomon came to my cell and opened the door. With a finger to his lips, he placed a hooded robe over my clothes and led me by the hand to his tent. I shivered like a puppy in a downpour. I could not speak, but held tightly to his arm.

He hid me in his bedroom and sat cross-legged before his fire. I can barely see to write these words, but if something should yet happen to me, I want them to be remembered. Sodomon seems to be waiting for something, or someone.

Lenore,

The monster, Dagog, has just come into the room with Sodomon. He assumes the name Assad, but I would know him anywhere. He sits at the fire, facing the entry door, his back to the room where I cower in the faint light of fading day, as Machato struggles valiantly to pour himself into the creeping darkness of the room so that I may write.

The room reeks with the odor of sulfur, and Assad's foul breath, like the stench of decaying flesh, sickens me. He is hunched over, reading something by the flames of Sodomon's fire. Parasite! He holds my death decree in his hands. How I want to rush into the room and leap on the monster, claw his beady eyes out of his head. I feel I will explode—sitting here, doing nothing, while this monster gloats over his victory.

Wait. He speaks. His voice creeps, like the sound of water beetles with their scratchy legs, scurrying over a hard surface. It sends chills up my spine.

"Has the sacrifice been prepared?" he asked.

"Yes." Sodomon is curt, unfriendly.

"She wears the ceremonial robe and face covering?"

"Yes."

"Then let us go and enjoy the offering." Assad's voice was pleased.

Just wait until the beast finds my cell empty! I wish I could see his face. Perhaps I will. Do I dare, Lenore, to mingle with the crowd and watch from a distance?

Lenore,

I have not written for over two weeks. I could not find words. Even now, my thoughts are like daggers—they cut me to the heart.

I did not know the price that was paid for my release or I could not—would not—have accepted. I did not know until Miammi told me, the day after I arrived at her house. When it was too late.

I will try, now, to write the words that must be written, but the pages will not be pretty, for already my tears smear the ink and smudge the thin pages.

Assad had been watching me, as I suspected, for some time. He knew that I was a Resister. I am not surprised. What I did not know was that he had issued a reward for my capture, offering a full pardon to any prisoner, regardless of their crime. To assure his success, he extended that pardon to ten others of the prisoner's choosing. There are some, even among the Resisters, who could be tempted to surrender me to Assad to save themselves and their families from the flames.

When Miammi told me this, I said, "Then my freedom is fickle. Assad will not withdraw his reward until I am captured again. An empty cell will serve only to increase his offer. At least (and I must confess that my next words were tinged with bitterness) my capture will purchase freedom for some condemned person."

My bitterness was abated with my next thought. Immon was betrayed for silver. Why should I expect better treatment at the hands of Dagog than the King himself had received?

Stop whining, I told myself.

Miammi's next words were like stones falling from the sky, hammering against my heart. They did not, at first, sink into my mind. I am so ashamed, so sorry that I am immensely shallow and judging of others.

"Nasha took your place."

"What...?"

Miammi nodded, then crossed the room and tried to wrap me in her arms, but I did not feel the need for comfort. Not yet. The words had no meaning for me. They were echoes, resounding upon my brain like words flung against a mountainside. I could not absorb them.

Miammi dropped her arms to her sides, the tears in her eyes brimming over.

"Sit down, Salina." She patted the bench beside her. Like one in a dream, I obeyed.

"Let me tell you about Nasha. After you left, she told me that she had been a fire dancer since the age of three. Three, Salina. Such a child. She did not want to dance. What child wants to be a part of something as vile and terrifying as the sacrificial fire? When she began, at the insistence of Assad, there were few executions, and even those that occurred were represented to Nasha as the just deaths of terrible criminals.

She told me about the first time a child was offered. Nasha was ten years old. She took the flowers from her hair, tossed the garland of orchids from around her waist into the fire, and walked away from the god of the night. She went to her father and begged to be released. He laughed at her. That was when she learned that Assad was not her natural father. Both her parents had been put to death when Nasha was two years old.

"Why? Why did he kill them?"

"Because he wanted their child. He wanted Nasha. He raised her to dance like no other, and he took great pride in her ability.

"When Nasha learned the truth, she walked about in shock for days. She could not eat or sleep. Finally, Assad forced her to take a mixture prepared by the shaman to 'calm her nerves.' It did not make her forget, but it made her numb to the pain. After she met you, she began to hope that you could help her. She sensed your allegiance to the Great King Immon, and she wanted to be like you.

"When Nasha came to us through the jungle she came for good. She said that she would rather die than return to the service of Dagog in the Land of Lasciviousness.

"The day that we learned of your capture, Bolati and ten other men were prepared to attempt a rescue. We knew there was little hope of success, but Bolati would have died in the attempt, if necessary. Then Nasha convinced him that she could persuade Sodomon to release you. I suppose we wanted to believe it. We did not know that she would give her life in return. She left you a letter."

Miammi held it out to me, and I took it and kissed it. Then I put it in my dress, and have carried it for the past two weeks. Perhaps I will read it tomorrow.

Lenore,

I have not yet read Nasha's letter. It will, I know, be bittersweet. The sweet I long to know, but even the sweet is bitter because I harbored such animosity toward one who loved me so much. I am a worm. I know that now.

Lenore,

Machato smiles once more. He has hidden his face from me this past fortnight. I could say that he does so because the winter rains have come, but I know that he is ashamed for me. Perhaps he has forgiven me, for streams of light pour from his pail of goodness and warm the rock I sit on. It is I who have yet to forgive myself.

Nasha, I will read your letter, not because I am worthy, but because to refrain is to disrespect one who deserves to be honored.

Lenore,

I read Nasha's letter yesterday. Today, I copy it here so that her words will never be forgotten. I have written them, also, on the tablet of my heart.

My Dearest Salina,

I am not good with words, as you are, but I must try to say what is in my heart.

You are the first person who ever loved me, as long as I can remember. Others have admired me for my dancing, or lusted after my beauty, but you alone loved me unselfishly and without reservation.

You did not reject me. You rejected what I have done—as do I. But I want to tell you what you have done for me. You taught me to respect myself, and that is why I had the courage to flee from Assad. You shared the truth with me, and I could no longer serve Dagog while sharing your love for the Great King Immon.

Assad would have found me, and he would have destroyed your family and the other Resisters, because that is what he does best. I could not be responsible for that, so I was faced with a decision: return to Assad on my own and resume dancing the dance of death, which was not really a choice because my feet would have refused to dance even if my mind commanded it, or take my own life willingly, and beseech the Great King Immon to accept me by his mercy and not by my goodness.

Miammi, whom I love as my own mother, assured me that the Great King Immon does not accept or reject us based on our goodness, but on our surrender to him, which I am most willing to do.

You cannot know how happy I am to exchange bondage to Dagog for death in the Kingdom of Adawm and an afterlife in the Other Kingdom. It sounds like a lovely place. That is why I went to Sodomon with my request. I suspected that he wanted to free you—and I gave him the means to do so. My death warrant is sealed either way—why not make it count for something?

As far as Assad is concerned, you are dead, and I cannot be found. It pleases me to think that I have escaped his hand, for truly, this is the only way that I could ever do so.

Know that I love you, and if there is anything to forgive, I do so wholeheartedly. You are my sister and my friend.

Love,
Nasha

PS: I look forward to seeing you in the Other Kingdom

Goodbye, my friend. I hope someday to be worthy of your love for me.

Lenore,

Yesterday, Bolati brought little Samia to see me. She is three years old and full of mischief. I can see Bolati in her face, and she has Miarrow's eyes. I could stare at her forever and never tire of it—but she would not like that, and besides she is never still for more than a moment. She calls me Auntie Lina. It's a pretty name, don't you think?

What am I going to do with myself, Lenore? I am a soldier at heart, trained for espionage, and broken in heart and spirit. There must be something useful I can do.

Lenore,

A strange thing happened—oh, I almost forgot to apologize—I haven't written for a few weeks. Nothing much has taken place, so I hope you will forgive me.

Yesterday, as I sat on the boulder near the river (I don't know why I do that to myself—it feels no better now than when I was eleven), I saw a small boat floating with the current. At first I was startled, then I recognized a friend, a messenger well known to all of us.

He waved and came ashore. He had news. "Sodomon is ill," he said. This was not good. "The shaman has been with him for the past twenty-four hours, but all of his concoctions seem to make Sodomon's condition grow worse."

I'll bet, I thought. This is Assad's doing. He is preparing a coup. The atrocities we will suffer under Assad's control will make Sodomon's reign look righteous in comparison.

I thanked the messenger and asked him to keep us posted on Sodomon's condition. He agreed to do so. I watch for him every day. It will not be long.

Lenore

I sit on the stone in my quiet place, watching the river run to the sea. The current is not swift, but it is sure—and it will remain true to its course. It is in our nature to do likewise. We do what we have always done, and what our fathers before us did. But what if a boulder is thrown into the river and the waters must flow around it? What happens to the river? Its course is changed, and eventually it will wear down the soil and form a new bed for itself, it will redirect its flow.

Perhaps Sodomon is as much a Resister as I am, Lenore. The course was set for the river of his life long before he had any say about it. He followed that course until the Messenger came and spoke the truth, bringing division in the Land of Lasciviousness.

A boulder was tossed into the river of lives that flows through the land. No longer was there undivided loyalty to the Prince of the Darkness, for the Great King Immon provided a better course, and with his help, we, the Resisters, have carved out a new riverbed.

Sodomon has been caught in the parting of the ways, and Assad has used this to his own advantage.

Lenore,

The door of my heart has opened wide and Machato has flooded its chambers with pure white light. I sing as I work, and smile like a schoolgirl. Hope has returned like the nesting birds in spring. A fire is rekindled inside me—a passion for life—that elusive thing that takes a drab existence and dresses it up for a party.

The messenger came today, rowing his small boat across the crocodile-infested waters. This is what he told us.

"Since I last came to this village, Sodomon grew worse. He lingered long at the door of death. The shaman could do no more, and gave the chief up for dead, though breath was still in him and his heart beat with a faint hammering against his chest. His eyes were glazed, and he could not speak. 'Leave him,' the shaman said, 'to die in peace.'"

But Sodomon did not die. Some say a great light shone from within his tent. All were afraid to go near. The chief cried out, 'Leave me alone! I am a wicked man,' but the light did not leave. Chief Sodomon rose from his bed and walked out into the forest by the pale light of the new moon. He has not been found among the living or the dead. Assad has many searchers looking for him, but all in vain."

Sodomon is coming here, Lenore. I know that he is.

Lenore,

I was baking bread when Chief Sodomon crossed the river. He swam across, yet no crocodile molested him. When Sodomon came out of the water, Machato beamed upon him with such intensity that the misting water, evaporating in the torrid heat, shimmered like a halo around his head.

He came toward us, his gaze averted, his shoulders bent. He knew we would not harm him, for our reputation is well known; our battles are fought by strategic planning, and we overcome our enemy with weapons forged not in the Kingdom of Adawm, but by the hand of the Great King Immon.

I dropped my pans and spoon immediately and went out to meet him. I stood face to face with him. He knelt on the soft grass at my feet and sobbed. I put my hands beneath his skinny elbows and raised him to his feet. "Can you forgive me?" he asked between great wrenching sobs that could have been heard at a great distance.

My people gathered around Sodomon, and some even reached out their hands to touch him. A touch of forgiveness, of compassion. Little Samia walked over to the sorrowing chief, having no idea who he was, and wrapped her small arms around his legs. Looking up at him, she said in her tiny voice, "I love you."

The tears flowed like rivers around the fire of the Resisters last night, and plans were made that we hoped would ease our suffering.

Lenore,

After three days, Beloti accompanied Chief Sodomon back to the Land of Lasciviousness. This time the chief was not required to swim across the Roan River with all its hungry crocodiles. He sat cross-legged in the bottom of Beloti's boat and waved to the people of my village who lined the water's edge and shouted farewell until a bend in the river hid him from our view. Little Samia took my hand and walked with me back to our dwelling. It was then that I saw tears in her eyes, as in my own. I picked her up and carried her in my arms. Goodbye is never easy, and none of us was sure that we would see Sodomon again this side of the Other Kingdom.

Lenore,

Beloti has just returned with news from the Land of Lasciviousness. You will not belive the courage of our old chief. He has issued a decree that says:

The Resisters and all others who reside in the Land of Lasciviousness are hereby declared free from all obligation to dance at the fire of the gods or to serve the Prince of the Darkness.

There is great rejoicing among the Resisters and all who sympathize with us.

Lenore,

I sit upon the stone, to which I have finally given a name. I call it IROC—In Remembrance of Christiano.

Miammi says that I am foolish to remember you so fondly, my dear friend. That I should forget. Often, I find that trying to forget certain things makes me remember them even more. Have you forgotten me, Christiano? I hope so. There is no need for both of us to suffer the sorrows of unrequited love. Am I melancholy today? Yes. By tomorrow I may not miss you.

It seems I have company. Sonora is coming my way with her three children. I will have to write later.

CHAPTER 7: AGE SIXTEEN

Lenore,

Today I am sixteen. A spinster. I cannot say that I am happy—happiness is reserved for small children who are still ignorant. But joy, the sweet sorrow of knowing that life, though filled with pain, is temporary, and that which lasts forever cannot be taken away from me, but is stored up in another, safer place. That certainty warms my heart and fills my soul with gladness deeper and richer than mere happiness. It is joy unspeakable and full of promise. That—no one can ever take away from Salina of the Land of Lasciviousness.

Lenore,

I am a watcher of children today. Sonora went to the marketplace with Thomas, her husband. I don't mind. I will sit on IROC and dream of old times.

The children romp with such energy! They are fair skinned like their mother, with eyes like deep mountain pools beneath a summer sky.

You bathe their faces in a golden stream, Machato, that bleaches their hair and

paints freckles on their noses.

Bonita is nine and as thin as I was at her age. Her brothers are twins, five years old and full of mischief. See, Lenore, they pull Bonita's braids and run away. She is getting angry now. She would pummel them if she could catch them. But she won't. They are much too fast.

They are with me almost every day. Sometimes, I forget that I have no children. Sometimes, but not often.

Lenore,

Machato sleeps late today behind his curtain of clouds. Perhaps he is being considerate of my young charges who played too long beneath his harsh stare yesterday and complained later of pink faces. Sonora scolded them for their carelessness, but they would do the same today if they had the opportunity. They won't, of course, because Sonora and Thomas are taking them along when they go to market today. They are going to see old friends who live in the political district.

I know that Sodomon's decree has been honored so far, but I do not trust it. Assad's power continues to grow and the citizens of the Land of Lasciviousness have changed little, except for our small band of Resisters. Some Resisters have even turned back to their old ways since moving back to their homes in the city.

I am going also, Lenore. Quick decisions are often bad ones, but what harm can it do, since I have been declared dead? A dead person should be safe in the streets

of the Land of Lasciviousness.

Lenore,

A quick note. The streets seem peaceful, but it is a restless quiet, like the peace in the eye of a storm. All is not as it seems. I am sure of it.

I am going to see Sodomon. He will tell me what I should know.

Lenore,

I sit before the fire in Sodomon's house. I have shared a small portion of my journal with him. I hope you do not mind. He asks that I record the words he is about to speak. I will honor his request. Sodomon says that I must hide if Assad comes to his door. We watch with careful eyes and listen even as we speak. He says that Assad has declared a holy war. I ask him to explain.

He says that Assad has been speaking in the marketplace and on street corners, even in the neighborhoods far from the political district. He has persuaded many that the Great King Immon is the enemy of all who live in the Land of Lasciviousness and that the Prince of the Darkness is our benevolent master.

These are the words of Assad as Sodomon repeats them to me:

The Land of Lasciviousness has always been a people of the night. Our fathers slept by day and played by night, and worked only when it was

unavoidable. We had no rules other than one, a prohibition against Oneida. Our fathers understood that what is right is one man's eyes is wrong in the eyes of another, and they meant to protect us from self-righteous do-gooders who would stand in judgment against our ways and deprive us of our pleasures.

The Resisters have criticized, judged, and condemned us because of their allegiance to the one they call the Great King Immon. We have not seen this royal person, and I assure you that he exists only in their proud imaginations. Those who claim to be his followers are aberrant citizens who refuse to join our feasts, dance at our fire, or conform to the principles upon which this great land is founded.

Therefore, I propose that we, as a people, refuse to honor the decree of a weak and insipid chief who bends to the will of those who would rob us of the pleasures shared by all rightful citizens of the Land of Lasciviousness.

I, Assad, will lead my people back to the traditions of our fathers—a righteous cause.

I hereby declare a just and holy war against all who oppose us, and I declare that all who are not with us are against us. We will deal with Resisters without mercy, and we will reclaim our land!

Lenore,

Rain drizzles from the broad leaves high above my head and trickles down my back. Using my skirts to create a makeshift shelter for myself and the three little ones sleeping curled up close together, I huddle beneath the cypress branches as I write these words.

Death walks boldly in the streets in the Land of Lasciviousness today. Assad and his death squads patrol with ruthless dedication.

I left Sodomon's house in a hurry yesterday, anxious to find Sonora and Thomas after hearing the words of the old chief. I walked as quickly as I dared to the house of their friend. I recognized it—the house of Orr, the most treacherous of Assad's generals. Orr had condemned more Resisters to the fire than any other of Assad's commanders.

No! I wanted to scream. This is a dream—a terrible dream! No more bloodshed, no more violent deaths. I lost all fear and ran toward the house. No one was home.

My stomach heaved, and I doubled over and lost my supper. "Please," I pleaded, hoping, I suppose, that King Immon would hear me from his throne room in the Other Kingdom and intervene in the affairs of the Kingdom of Adawm, as he has before. How could I bear another loss—and one so great as this? I don't know how I knew, but I did. Somehow, I did.

I ran to the place of sacrifice. The fires to the god of the night flamed high against the darkening sky. Standing within a few feet of the blaze, Thomas and Sonora and the children huddled close together, surrounded by seven fire dancers.

The dancers were shouting and shaking clenched fists in the faces of the condemned. Their bodies glistened in the amber flames that shot upward to lick the dark clouds where Machita hid her face and shed thin tears that sizzled against the glowing coals beneath.

Thomas and Sonora's hands were tied with thick ropes behind their backs. The children clung to their parents, refusing to be separated from them.

Two hulking forms emerged from the shadows. I swear they were not men, but near-human creatures with strangely formed bodies and pale, twisted faces. They grabbed Thomas and Sonora and tossed them like kindling on top of the flaming logs in the center of the fire.

My knees buckled, and I longed to surrender to the darkness that enveloped me, yield to it and sink to the ground. Assad's followers would be sure to recognize me, and I would join my friends in the fire. A welcome relief.

Then I realized that the children were crying. Bonita screamed for her mother, and the twins squealed wordlessly, a pitiful wail that I will never forget.

The fire dancers were holding the children to the ground, wrapping ropes around their wrists and arms, cutting into their tender flesh.

I stood in the shadows, grinding my teeth, my nails biting into my palms. I would have rushed upon the dancers and shoved as many as I could into the fire, but hope restrained me.

A voice whispered in my ear, "I have come to set the captives free."

Immon? The voice that spoke these words was not of the Kingdom of Adawm. I

am sure of it, for I heard it from within. The Messenger spoke often of the person within—the spirit-person that cannot be confined or destroyed—the part of us that will live forever. That is the part of me that heard these words, and they sustained me. I stood still, and waited.

Suddenly, Chief Sodomon barreled into the midst of the fire dancers, knocking two of them off their feet. The others backed off, and the children edged away from the fire, blending into the crowd in the confusion that followed.

I elbowed my way through the dense crowd of spectators and gathered the twins into my arms. A man standing nearby surprised me by lifting Bonita in his arms and looking at me with eyebrows raised, whispering, "Where shall we take them?" I nodded toward Sodomon's tent, and after a moment's hesitation, he sprinted toward it. He raised the flap of the tent and looked quickly around. Seeing that no one was present, he deposited Bonita on a rug in a corner and promptly turned and left. A sympathizer. Never had I been more grateful than at that moment.

With a finger to my lips, I motioned the children to be quiet, then lifted the tent flap, and watched in astonishment as Sodomon raced over to the great rain barrel that stood nearby, and pushed the cart into the fire. The wooden barrel disintegrated—and the fire went out. For the first time in the history of the land, the fire that burned to honor the Prince of the Darkness went out!

A roar of anger rose up from the villagers. Shrieking and shouting, the dancers converged on the old chief. He saw me standing in the shadows and his eyes met mine. My last memory of Sodomon is locked into my mind forever, for his eyes shone with a joy not of this world. He straightened his shoulders as if

relieved of a heavy load, and lifted his hand in a half-wave just before the crowd overtook him. Gawkers cheered them on as they carried him to the circle of death.

They put him through the gauntlet, beating him with wooden sticks, hurling stones, and kicking him when he fell. He did not cry out or curse his tormentors. He held his hands out and seemed to speak to someone that none of us could see. Dear Sodomon, I will see you in the Other Kingdom.

Lenore,

The children are asleep in Sodomon's tent. I moved them to the bedroom, where I hope we will all remain undetected. I cannot take them home tonight. None of us has strength for the journey.

I am puzzled over the man who helped me rescue the children. Who is he? I did not see his face clearly in all the smoke and confusion. Will I ever see him again? I would like to thank him.

Lenore,

Someone left a letter inside the door of Sodomon's tent before first light this morning. It has my name on it. Someone in the city knows who I am, someone who does not want me to know who he is. We may be in danger even as I write. I am curious about the letter. I think I will open it before the children awaken.

Lenore,

My heart aches today with both sorrow and joy. I grieve over the death of my friends, and I worry about the children, but I am happy all the same, because of the letter that I hold in my hand.

It says Christiano lives. He lives!

I will tell you more after I care for the children. I must get them out of Sodomon's house today.

Lenore,

A ship came into the harbor today just as Machato attired himself in his finest robes of gold and amber. He torched the heavens, and fiery fingers of light flared across the blue waters of the sky. Two men launched a rowboat into the waters of the bay. They are coming ashore.

I watch from behind the flap of Sodomon's tent. I am desperate for an opportunity to get the children out of here. They are all awake and move about a bit, though slowly and with sad faces. We dare not brave the streets just yet. Something will happen soon to distract all eyes away from us. I am sure of it.

These men, they are in the service of the Great King Immon. They speak of him to the fire dancers.

Trouble breaks out. The men are under attack. They run for their boat.

Let's go. Now, children! This is our chance.

Lenore,

We are safe, at last, aboard the good ship *Seeking*. I remember this ship. It is the vessel that carried the Messenger to my people. The children are tucked into bed in the galley, and I am too tired to sleep. I will go above deck and say goodbye to the land of my birth. Perhaps I can get a message to Miammi that I am safe at last.

VOCABULARY AND PRONUNCIATION KEY

CHARACTER   PRONUNCIATION

Addar   ə-'där\
Emperor over all kingdoms and ruler of the world.

Immon   i-'män\
Son of the emperor and king of the Other Kingdom.

Miarrow   \mē\'är\ō\
Salina's father.

Miammi   \mē\ 'äm\ē\
Salina's mother.

Salina   \sə-'lē-nə\
A child who met the Messenger at nine years old.

Messenger (the Messenger)   \'mes-ĕn-jər\
Emissary of King Immon.

Sodomon   \'sä-də-mən\
Sodomon is chief over the Land of Lasciviousness.

Machato \mə\'chä\tō\
Salina's name for the sun.

Machita \mə\'chē\tə\
Salina's name for the moon.

Helgotha \hĕl\'gŏ)\thə\
Salina's name for the stone that she liked to sit on to write in her diary.

Sashay \'să\shā\
A child who comes to Salina's village.

Demensi \dĕ\'mĕn\sē\
Salina's brother (older than her but younger than Beloti).

Beloti \bə\'lŏ\tē\
Salina's oldest brother.

Surice \sŭ/'rēs\
Elder and leader of the Resisters.

Christiano \kris\tē\'ä\nō
A boy who comes to the village.

Stephanie \'stĕ\făn\ē\
Christiano's sister.

Pathalos \pă\'thă\lōs\
A physician who is friendly to the Resisters.

Prince of the Darkness, also called **Dagog** \'dā\gŏg\
A form-changer who can appear as a Dragon or a person—enemy of all who serve Immon.

Assad \ə\'säd\
Counselor to Chief Sodomon.

Sonora \sŏ\'nor\ə\
Salina's personal secretary.

DeMaile \dĕ\'māl\
An associate of Salina.

Nasha \'nä\shə\
A friend of Salina.

Samia \săm\'ē\ə\
Salina's niece.

OTHER WORDS PRONUNCIATION

Lasciviousness \lə-'si-vē-əs\'nes\
Lewd, without restraint.

Resister \ri-'zis-tər\
One who resists. Especially one who actively resists the authority of a government.

In the Land of Lascivious, a Resister was one who resisted the demands of the Ancient Creed of the Land because it violated their moral and spiritual standards.

Oneida \ō\'nī\də\
(1) the only crime punishable by death in the Land of Lasciviousness;
(2) taking a stand against practices you disagree with.

COMING SOON

The Second Book of Journeys

Mikhail, a former merchant, joined the First Journey when his ship, *Good Works*, foundered on rocks in the Sea of Life. Now ashore in a strange and ravaged land, he is being pursued by the evil dragon, Dagog. Mikhail would not be afraid of the hideous creature seeking his destruction—if only he could see the mighty and invisible warriors that defend him. He mistakenly believes that he travels alone and loneliness threatens to consume him, especially when he remembers the days of old when he sailed the seas with his beloved Anastasia.

Still, Mikhail is committed to the Quest for the Other Kingdom. His journey leads him down treacherous trails and often places him in harm's way. Intrigue abounds in the shadowed woods and Mikhail stumbles into the arms of the enemy on more than one occasion. Entrapment is Dagog's specialty. Will his diabolical schemes destroy the merchant who has dared to venture into his territory?

ABOUT THE AUTHOR

Born in Newport, Arkansas, Linda Settles spent the first years of her life in a three-room house across the road from a cotton patch. The family had all the necessary commodities, an outhouse, chickens, and a dilapidated Ford. Linda was the oldest daughter, and her brother, Eddie (eleven months older than she), was her best friend and protector. When Eddie died at age nine, Linda suddenly became the eldest in a family that grew until there were six children, an absentee mother, and a domineering father.

Linda has always loved writing. As a teenager she wrote poetry that was often published in Latchstrings, a newspaper in North Little Rock. Having noticed her poems, the head of Poet's Roundtable of Arkansas offered her an honorary position in the Roundtable with a view to mentoring her, and invited her to their annual banquet to be introduced. Linda's father refused to let her attend, but she didn't give up writing. She wrote a poem about real estate that the Arkansas Democrat newspaper used to launch its real estate section. Linda was photographed and written up in the first edition.

Linda grew up and fled the Ozarks for Michigan, where she discovered how wonderful life is when one is free to enjoy it. She soon met and married Michael Settles. Linda and Mike are excited about the direction their life has taken and are thrilled to write each new chapter in the book of their personal Journey on the Sea of Life. There is much to be done before they reach the Other Kingdom, and they look forward to doing it.

EDICT HOUSE PUBLISHING GROUP, LLC

PHILOSOPHY STATEMENT

Remember the king's edict in the story of Esther? King Xerxes had signed a decree assuring the annihilation of the Jewish people. The decree could not be rescinded, though Xerxes regretted it, for he had sealed it with his royal signet ring. The Jews were saved by Mordecai's suggestion that they be allowed to arm themselves. Xerxes issued an edict granting the Jews in every city the rights to assemble and to protect themselves and their families.

We live in an era when the values that sustain the health of our nation and our lives are challenged on all sides. History records the age-old question "What is truth?" The answer requires a lifelong search. Every individual has the right and the responsibility to speak the truth as he or she perceives it, for absolute truth is our only defense against the destruction of our values and our lives.

We at Edict House Publishing Group, LLC are committed to publishing books that will facilitate the search for truth as they encourage, enlighten, and entertain our readers.

ACKNOWLEDGMENTS

Karla, my awesome copyeditor who firmly adheres to the old adage "challenge everything," and makes every book better because of it.

§

Cynthia Frank my always mentor and friend, and the staff at Cypress House.

§

All my friends and family who have taken the time to read my work and offer their insights.